PEEK-A-BOO!

101 Ways to Make a Baby Smile

Written by Sheila Hanly

To: ....

From: ....

*Babies love to explore new things and this delightful book is full of activities to keep your
baby busy and happy. But, as every parent knows, babies should never be left to play unattended
as there are many things, such as pets, plants, or water, that can be hazardous to babies.*

DORLING KINDERSLEY

London • New York • Moscow • Sydney

Good morning, Baby

1 A good
morning kiss.

2 Stick out
your tongue.

3 Up you get!

4 Whee, you can fly.

5 Squeeze my cheeks.

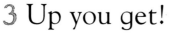

6 Lots of hugs ... and hugs ... and hugs.

7 Let's rub heads.　　8 Where's Daddy gone? Peek-a-boo!

Let's get dressed

9 On with your shirt.

10 Where have you gone?

11 There you are!

12 Nibble your fingers.

13 Eat you all up.

14 Suck your toes. 15 Pop on a sock. 16 Look in the mirror.

17 Try on a hat. Pull it off? Put it on.

18 Pull my hair. 19 Count your fingers. 20 Count your toes.

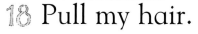

Let's play

21 Swing high.

22 Swing low.

23 Get ready to race ...

steady now.

24 A tug-of-war.   25 Who is in the box?   26 Let's dance.

27 Bounce on
my knees.

28 Swing on
my foot.

29 Let's clap
hands.

30 Off you go!

Making a noise

31 Blow the trumpets.

32 Bash a saucepan.

33 Squeeze Duckie, squeak, squeak!

34 Whizz goes the top.

35 Play a tune on the piano.

36 Shake that
rattle.

37 Ding, dong on
the xylophone.

38 Can you hear
the music?

39 Ring the bells,
ting-a-ling.

40 Bang, bang, bang,
beat the drum.

Let's play quietly

41 Listen to the clock, tick tock, tick tock.

42 Tickle you with a feather.

43 Here comes a big spider to ...

tickle your tummy!

44 Round and round the garden like a teddy bear

45 Watch the mobile spin.

46 Can you hear Kitty purr?

47 Make messy hand prints.

48 Where is Teddy hiding?

Here he is!

49 Listen to my heart go thump, thump.

Playing with toys

50 Concentrate now. Stack the rings.

51 Bang in the shapes.

52 Up pops the jack-in-a-box.

53 Hello! Here's a puppet show.

54 Rub noses with Teddy.

55 Chase the ball.

56 A teddy bears' tea party.

57 Pop the bricks in the basket.

58 Vroom, vroom with the truck.

59 Let's build a tower of bricks.

60 Knock it down again!

Let's explore

61 Look! Puppy wants to play.

62 She loves me, she loves me not.

63 Smell the flower.

64 Dig with a spade.

65 Try to catch bubbles.

66 Watch a fluttery butterfly.

67 Fill a bucket with sand.

68 Help make a sandcastle.

69 Take Teddy for a ride.

70 Water the plants.

Out and about

71 A piggyback ride.

72 Wave bye-bye.

73 Look at the birdie.

74 Whoosh!

75 Are you ready for a
ride in your pushchair?

Down the slide you go.   **76** Throw bread to the duck.

Time to eat

78 Chew on a bread-stick.

77 Try feeding yourself.   79 Drink milk from your bottle.

80 Munch a banana.

81 Nibble a biscuit.

82 Bang that spoon.

83 Here comes a plane, open wide.

Bathtime fun

84 Make a little bubble beard ... and a bubble bath hat.

85 Bob, bob, bob go the bath boats.

86 Pour water from a beaker.

87 Wind up the turtle.

88 Squeeze that sponge.

89 Give your face a good clean.

90 Make a big splash.

91 Oops! You've dropped Duckie.

Found him again!

92 Cuddle dry in a towel.

93 A puff of powder.

Goodnight, Baby

94 Look at a book.

95 Let's read a bedtime story.

96 Say "Night, night" to Teddy.

97 A bedtime drink.

98 Give me a big goodnight cuddle.

99 Whistle a lullaby.

100 Let's snooze together.

Fast asleep

101 Sleep tight, Baby.

DK

A DORLING KINDERSLEY BOOK

Art Editor
Mandy Earey
Deputy Managing Editor
Dawn Sirett
Deputy Managing Art Editor
Sarah Wright-Smith
Production
Josie Alabaster

Photography Steve Shott
Illustrations Carol Hill

Published in Great Britain by
Dorling Kindersley Limited,
9 Henrietta Street, London WC2E 8PS

2 4 6 8 10 9 7 5 3 1

Visit us on the World Wide Web at http://www.dk.com

Copyright © 1998 Dorling Kindersley Limited, London

A CIP catalogue record for this book is
available from the British Library.

ISBN 0-7513-5853-3

Colour reproduction by Colourscan, Singapore
Printed in Hong Kong by Wing King Tong

Additional photography by
Jane Burton, Jo Foord, Dave King,
Karl Shone, and Kim Taylor.

Dorling Kindersley would like to thank Quadro for
the use of their climbing frame and the
following who were photographed for this book:

Paul Alcock, Autumn and Yolanda Amajoutt,
Claire Barratt, Christian Cadwallader, Jacob Cole,
Antonio and Valentia Costa, Ellis Coulson, Edward Davison,
Caroline and Courtney Delahunty, Tommy Dixon,
Remi Fawcus-Williams, Daniel France, Ella Franklinos,
Danny and Lewis Gibson, Polly Gwinnett, Alex Holcombe,
Kiki Humphries, James Miller, Pui Ming Chow, Alexandra Murray,
Kay and Leah Musisi, Amy and Kyle Ogata, Katie Peddar,
Marco Pini, Charlie Pyecraft, Abby Rakic-Platt,
Maximillien Solom, Oliver Stewart, Ellie and Lesley Thomas,
Piers Tilbury, and Pascal Toresse.